30 DAYS TO...
YES TO ME

The Power of Know:

Be Kind, Nurturing, Optimistic, and Worthy to Self.

ANOUK MCINTYRE

Disclaimer

The information presented herein represents the author's view as of the publication date. Because of the rate with which conditions change, the author reserves the right to alter and update his opinion based on the new conditions. The book is for informational purposes only. While every attempt has been made to verify the information provided in this book neither the author nor his affiliates/partners assume any responsibility for errors, inaccuracies, or omissions. Any slights of people or organizations are unintentional. If advice concerning legal or related matters is needed, the services of a fully qualified professional should be sought. This book is not intended for use as a source of legal or accounting advice. You should be aware of any laws that govern business transactions or other business practices in your country and state. Any reference to any person or business whether living or dead is purely coincidental.

Dedication

To all the brave souls
on a journey of self-discovery

May this book be a guiding light on your path to self-love. May you find the courage to embrace your unique beauty, to nurture your inner strength, and to love yourself unconditionally. May you remember the Power of KNOW: Be Kind, Nurturing, Optimistic, and Worthy to Self. This book is dedicated to you.

Table of Contents

Foreword

S elf-love is an innate ability to explore one's inner gifts of transformative power, spirit, intimacy, awareness, flaws, uniqueness, and faith, a profound act of generosity delivered to each of us at birth by the almighty.

At a time where the demands of life and the attention of the world require our constant validation the profound and transformative power of self-love protects one's peace and sanity. This book is a guiding testament to a deliberate journey of embracing your inner being of love and worth. Self-love is a journey, an exploration of the inner soul, a pilgrimage of understanding and honoring worth, a gift to oneself whereby accepting yourself wholly and unconditionally along with all your perfect imperfections.

The essence of self-love transcends mere acceptance. It is a celebration of our uniqueness, our flaws, and our aspirations. Self-love is not just a feeling; it is the cornerstone upon which life's fulfillments are built.

The pages that follow are a mosaic of perspectives woven together to inspire, encourage, and guide you on your pilgrimage toward self-love. In the chapters ahead, you will delve into the importance of setting boundaries, reflecting on acceptance and forgiveness, and knowing and feeling the beauty of the spirit within. Through triumphs and resilience, you will find solace and motivation in the pages that lie ahead. Let these words serve as a beacon of hope, encouragement, and fulfillment as you embark on a journey to profound and liberating self-love.

Yours on this journey,

Ronald McIntyre

Introduction

W hat is self-love? Consider it as an aspiration to prioritize and honor our well-being. When you harbor self-love, you show esteem for yourself. The essence lies in treating yourself with the same kindness you would extend to someone you deeply care about.

Yet, many of us have been taught to believe that we ought to prioritize others before ourselves. This often masquerades as concern for others or a display of modesty. Nevertheless, this approach is counterproductive. When you neglect to prioritize yourself, you limit your capacity to contribute to others effectively.

"Self-love is the foundation upon which we build our truest and most authentic selves, for in embracing our worth, we unlock endless possibilities for growth and happiness."

Since you spend every minute of the day with yourself, why not find joy in your own company?

Explore the following topics to cultivate self-love and appreciation so that you know to KNOW:

1. **Chapter 1:** How do you Measure Your Self-worth? Employing the right criteria makes a significant difference.

It's common to assess ourselves based on societal norms, but this can be a misguided approach.

2. **Chapter 2:** Embarking on a 30-day Journey to Self-Love. Numerous experts suggest that it takes 30 days to establish a habit. Cultivating effective habits is instrumental in achieving your desired outcomes. Over 30 days, you can achieve significant progress and build the momentum necessary for a substantial breakthrough in your self-love.

3. **Chapter 3:** Short Stories. Embark on a journey that explores the profound impact of self-love on our lives through diverse characters and experiences and witness the transformative power that arises when individuals embrace self-love in its various forms.

4. **Chapter 4:** Self-Love Affirmations. Explore the transformative power of positive self-talk with some affirmations designed to uplift, inspire, and cultivate a deep sense of self-love and unconditional self-acceptance.

5. **Chapter 5:** Conclusion. This marks the initial steps on your journey toward genuine self-love and self-esteem. What lies ahead on your path?

"The impact you make on people is not measured by the
numbers or the noise, but by the ripples of kindness,
understanding, and inspiration
that forever shape their lives"

Chapter 1

How Do You
Measure Your SelfWorth?

H ow, do you assess your self-worth? Is it tied to your financial status, your ability to fit into certain clothing, or possessing a prestigious job and a luxury car? It's a thought-provoking question. Many of us have a vague sense of whether we should love ourselves based on our life circumstances.

A valuable perspective to consider is how you would want your child to gauge their self-worth.

Would you encourage them to love themselves based on factors such as:

- Being wealthy or poor?

- Being more attractive than the average person?

- Experiencing more failures than successes?

- Achieving more successes than failures?

Do any of these factors warrant a child loving themselves more or less? What criteria would you use to determine their self-worth?

Do you think any of these factors should influence a child's self-love positively or negatively? What standards would you employ to evaluate their sense of self-worth?

Factors that probably should not influence your level of self-love:

1. Education: If your child chooses a career path like welding or preschool teaching instead of attending college, should that diminish their worth? Pursue higher education if it aligns with your aspirations, but not attending college should not be a source of guilt.

2. Body shape or attractiveness: While diet and exercise contribute to your appearance, genetics play a significant role in traits like eye color, height, and body shape. Just as you wouldn't think less of a loved one for changes in their appearance, you shouldn't judge yourself harshly for not resembling a fitness model or movie star.

3. Career: Some professions are more demanding or lucrative, but life encompasses more than high stakes careers. You're succeeding if you find fulfillment, can cover your expenses, and have time and resources for things you love.

4. Financial situation: Happiness is a more meaningful pursuit than wealth. Studies suggest that beyond a certain income threshold, additional wealth doesn't significantly boost happiness. Your income doesn't dictate your self-love; many remarkable individuals achieved greatness without amassing considerable wealth.

5. Possessions: Obsession with material possessions is noticeable in certain cultures. Comparing possessions can be an unwinnable battle. Recognize that happiness often transcends material wealth, as evidenced by people in less affluent countries rating themselves as happier.

6. Successes and failures: Everyone experiences triumphs and setbacks. View failures as opportunities to learn and grow. Many highly successful individuals have faced significant failures. Embrace your ability to persevere and learn from challenges.

7. Social connections: The worth of self-love isn't determined by the people you know or don't know. External relationships shouldn't be the basis for evaluating your self-worth; the term "self" underscores the internal nature of this assessment.

This list may appear challenging, as these are qualities highly valued in our culture. However, if you aspire to cultivate self-love, it's crucial to employ meaningful criteria.

Loving yourself hinges on understanding who you are and progressing toward becoming a person you genuinely respect. Recognizing your inherent uniqueness is a significant step in this journey.

The other essential component involves witnessing consistent personal growth. Humans thrive when making advancements, and you have the authority to define the direction of your progress. Engage in meaningful pursuits aligned with your values, and you'll find greater satisfaction in yourself.

While societal norms may dictate certain priorities, your self-worth transcends geographical locations. Whether you reside in Ukraine, Hawaii, or Australia, your essence remains unchanged. Society lacks the authority to grant or revoke your permission to love yourself; that power resides within you.

> "Not only are you entitled to embrace and express your individuality freely, but you also carry a moral obligation to do so."

How do you see yourself? What is your self-love and self-esteem rating?

_____

_____

_____

_____

_____

_____

_____

_____

_____

_____

_____

_____

_____

_____

_____

_____

_____

Chapter 2

Embarking On A
30-Day Journey to Self-Love

I t's sufficient for shedding a few pounds, increasing your pushup count, refining your tennis swing, or even mastering a simple tune on the violin.

This time frame is also significant for enhancing your capacity to love yourself. In just 30 days, you can uncover the wonderful aspects of your being. Furthermore, this period allows you to embark on the journey of treating yourself with kindness and initiating the path of self-improvement. Importantly, this self-improvement is not tied to acquiring societal accolades but revolves around evolving into the person you deeply admire.

Many of these activities can be integrated into your daily routine, emphasizing the importance of forming habits. Self-love is, to a large extent, a product of your habits, and cultivating the right ones will yield the desired outcomes.

While a few tasks may not be practical daily, especially for those with active schedules, consider incorporating them weekly or monthly.

Think of this as a 30-day self-love challenge. Approach it with an open mind and the courage to see it through. You'll likely find immense satisfaction in the results and yield to the Power of KNOW: Be Kind, Nurturing, Optimistic and Worthy to Self.

On your Mark, Get Set, Go: Establish your Commitment

A chieving a goal becomes significantly easier when you have a clear intention. Your vegetable garden wasn't planted last summer by chance—it happened because you intended to plant it. The same principle holds here.

Don't let the next 30 days slip away without purpose. Make a conscious decision to focus on enhancing your self-love and self-esteem during this month. Commit to giving it your best effort. Altering your daily routine can be challenging, but considering the progress you aim to achieve, it's well worth the effort.

Your success in this endeavor hinges on your intention and unwavering determination.

"Embracing a healthy self-love means we no longer feel the need to justify our actions or decisions, both to ourselves and others."

What is your commitment to yourself?

_____

_____

_____

_____

_____

_____

_____

_____

_____

_____

_____

_____

_____

_____

_____

Day 1:
Cultivate Awareness

P rogress can be elusive without a clear understanding of your current state.

Take a moment to observe how you treat yourself and draw a comparison with how you treat your friends and family.

It's common for many of us to exhibit more patience, understanding, and tolerance toward others than we do toward ourselves. Strikingly, we often extend greater kindness to strangers than we do to ourselves.

Pay attention to specific areas of self-treatment over the next 30 days:

- Self-talk

- Your emotional response to your mistakes compared to others' mistakes

- The impact of your treatment on your motivation to be your best

- Whether you treat yourself with a sense of importance and respect

- The habitual nature of your thoughts and actions toward yourself

- Cultivate a heightened awareness of your attitudes and behaviors toward yourself during this next month

"True Self -Love begins with a profound self-awareness."

Self-Reflection Notes

_____

_____

_____

_____

_____

_____

_____

_____

_____

_____

_____

_____

_____

_____

_____

_____

_____

Day 2:
Embrace Every
Compliment You Receive

Receiving compliments can be challenging when self-love is in short supply. Do you find it awkward when someone praises you? While embracing humility is commendable, it's also acceptable to derive joy from compliments.

From this moment forward, embrace every compliment that comes your way. A simple smile and a thank-you are sufficient. Remind yourself that you deserve the acknowledgment and resist the urge to deflect it.

"Some people deceive themselves as much by presuming that their flaws are always on the forefront of other people's minds."

Self-Reflection Notes

_____

_____

_____

_____

_____

_____

_____

_____

_____

_____

_____

_____

_____

_____

_____

_____

_____

_____

Day 3:
Begin Delving into a
Book on Self-Love

For the remainder of the 30 days, spend at least 15 minutes each day reading a book on the topic of self-love. If you get finished, start a new book. In place of a book, read an article online. Find a credible source and learn all you can about the importance and the process of self-love.

Regardless of where you acquire information, take some time to reflect on what you've learned. Consider how you can integrate this newfound knowledge into your daily life.

> "Reading about Self-Love is like opening a book to your own heart. In the pages of self-discovery, you find the wisdom to love and cherish the remarkable story that is you."

Self-Reflection Notes

_____

_____

_____

_____

_____

_____

_____

_____

_____

_____

_____

_____

_____

_____

_____

_____

_____

_____

Day 4:
Develop and Employ Affirmations

Affirmations require time to yield results, so, fortunately, you have several weeks ahead to harness their power. Through consistent repetition, you can instill a belief in almost anything—advertisers rely on this principle, evident in our extensive purchasing habits.

To effectively reprogram your subconscious for increased self-love, follow these daily strategies:

- Formulate 10 affirmations tailored to address self-love, considering the heightened awareness you've developed about your behaviors and attitudes toward yourself. Ensure your affirmations are positive and straightforward. For instance, "I love myself completely" serves as a suitable affirmation.

- Keep your affirmations readily accessible. Whether on your phone, in a compact notebook, or on an index card, choose a format you'll consistently carry with you.

- Engage with your affirmations multiple times a day. Take advantage of spare moments to read them, either to yourself or aloud when appropriate. Commence and conclude your day with a dedicated focus on your affirmations.

"After years of self-criticism yielding unsatisfactory results, why not embark on a new path? Give yourself the gift of approval and witness the transformative power it can have on your life."

Self-Reflection Notes

Day 5:
Engage in an Activity You've Always Desired

I ndulge in a small treat for yourself today. Whether it's experiencing a hot stone massage, trying a new restaurant, or learning to ride a motorcycle – take a moment to reflect on your desires. Once decided, go ahead and bring that desire to life. If it's more suitable for the weekend, solidify your plans for the activity and commit to them.

"Embrace the beauty of new adventures, for within their exploration, you'll find the blossoms of self-love unfolding in every step, creating a masterpiece of discovery and joy."

Self-Reflection Notes

Day 6:
Appreciate Your Physical Self

While you might not boast a sixpack, may have accumulated a few wrinkles, and now sport bifocals, these are minor details compared to the incredible capabilities your body still possesses. Even if your health is less than optimal, your body can still accomplish remarkable feats.

Take a moment to appreciate the often-overlooked aspects:

- **Sensory Abilities:** The capacity to see, hear, smell, touch, and taste. Reflect on the immense pleasure these senses bring.

- **Motor Skills:** The ability to walk and talk. Ponder the multitude of amazing experiences made possible by these fundamental abilities.

- **Life Creation:** Perhaps you've brought children into the world.

Even if you perceive your body as less aesthetically pleasing, its enduring abilities far outweigh such concerns. When you consider the multitude of things your body can still achieve, the superficial aspects become inconsequential.

"Cherish every curve, contour, scar, and imperfection; they are a testament to the unique and incredible journey of your existence."

Self-Reflection Notes

Day 7:
Maintain a Healthy Diet

P rove to yourself that you love your body by treating it like a king or queen for a day. Instead of giving in to your regular habits and impulses, eat nutritiously for just one day.

Feel free to continue for the remainder of the month or even the rest of your life.

"I embrace the notion that being cared for by myself is more than enough."

Self-Reflection Notes

Day 8:
Compose a Love Letter to Yourself

P icture having the most ideal friend or partner. Now, compose a letter to yourself as if it were from that person. Infuse it with love and encouragement. You can choose to write it on paper, send an email to yourself, leave a heartfelt voicemail, or any method you prefer. This might even become a rewarding daily practice for you.

"Write a letter to the extraordinary soul within. Let your own words become the love story your heart desires."

Self-Reflection Notes

Day 9:
Request a Favor from Someone

Individuals lacking in self-love often hesitate to inconvenience others. However, seeking assistance is not a burden. Just as you would willingly help someone else, it's reasonable to expect that others would be glad to assist you. Recognize your significance and acknowledge that it's okay to seek help when needed.

Identify something for which you could use assistance and approach an appropriate person for help. Begin with small requests to gradually build your comfort level.

"For in acknowledging your needs, you honor your worthiness within."

Self-Reflection Notes

_____

_____

_____

_____

_____

_____

_____

_____

_____

_____

_____

_____

_____

_____

_____

_____

_____

_____

Day 10:
Let Go of the Pursuit of Perfection

Whether you expect perfection from yourself, others, or both, the outcome is consistent misery. Perfection is an elusive concept that remains theoretical and unattainable.

Even if you think you've found the perfect person, it's an illusion. Perfection lies beyond the horizon of unseen imperfections.

Insisting on perfection from yourself ensures perpetual dissatisfaction and self-resentment. Setting unattainable standards is a surefire path to perpetual discontent.

Extend kindness to yourself and recognize that your best effort is sufficient. Today, free yourself from the burden of striving for perfection.

> "I have found that the main reason people struggle to embrace self-compassion is the fear of becoming self-indulgent. There is a mistaken belief that self-criticism is necessary to maintain discipline. However, this perception is largely influenced by societal norms, which erroneously promote the idea that being hard on oneself is the path to achievement."

Self-Reflection Notes

Day 11:
Organize Your Living Space

Most of us have way too much stuff in our homes. It creates stress and doesn't leave enough room for anything new to come into our lives. Cleaning and decluttering aren't necessarily fun, but it does provide a sense of control.

A clean, tidy environment is good for your selfesteem and peace of mind. Start with a single room today and branch out from there. Just a few minutes of decluttering each day can make a huge difference. Learn to keep things neat rather than waiting until the situation becomes unbearable before you act.

Know that you deserve to live in a pleasant environment.

"Organizing your surroundings is a dance of selflove, where every tidy corner becomes part of a harmonious symphony."

Self-Reflection Notes

Day 12:
Streamline Your Daily Agenda

How much time do you spend doing things you don't want to do?

Okay, we all must do things we don't want to do, but there are things you don't want to do that you don't have to do. It might be serving on the Parent-Teacher Organization or playing on the company softball team.

Look at your average month and list the activities that you don't enjoy. Yes, you still must pay your bills, but there are at least a few things on that list that you don't have to do.

So, don't do them. Let the appropriate people know, and then use that time for something that you do enjoy. Your happiness and time are important.

> "Streaming the melody of your daily agenda is an act of self-love, orchestrating the notes of intention, purpose, and self-care."

Self-Reflection Notes

_____

_____

_____

_____

_____

_____

_____

_____

_____

_____

_____

_____

_____

_____

_____

_____

_____

_____

_____

_____

_____

_____

Day 13:
Create a Plan for Managing Stress

M any persistent challenges in life often stem from ineffective stress management. Issues like reckless spending, overeating, missed opportunities, and more can often be traced back to a lack of effective stress coping mechanisms.

Developing a healthy and efficient approach to handling stress can yield remarkable benefits in your life. Consider incorporating these healthy options into your stress management toolkit:

1. **Meditation:** An ancient practice, meditation has never been more popular and can offer profound benefits.

2. **Exercise:** A brief jog or a few pushups not only boosts your mood but is also beneficial for your overall well-being.

3. **Connect with a friend:** Reach out to someone who cares; a supportive friend can often provide comfort and perspective.

4. **Let it go:** Practice releasing your stress, much like shedding a heavy suitcase with regular practice.

5. **Seek solutions:** If the cause of your stress is manageable, focus on finding a solution rather than dwelling on the stress itself.

Be mindful of when stress arises and experiment with these strategies. Feel free to explore other effective ideas that resonate with you.

"Mastering the art of stress management is a compassionate gift to self."

Self-Reflection Notes

_____

_____

_____

_____

_____

_____

_____

_____

_____

_____

_____

_____

_____

_____

_____

_____

_____

Day 14:
Compile a List of Things You are Grateful For

E ven if you find yourself without friends and living on a park bench, there are still aspects of your life to be grateful for. If you're not enduring nights in the rain, your list of reasons for happiness expands even further.

Our culture tends to accentuate the negative rather than the positive. Those who travel extensively often observe that people from North America frequently discuss what they dislike. In contrast, individuals from other cultures tend to focus on the things they appreciate.

You can shape your own miniature culture by choosing to concentrate on the positives in your life.

Therefore, your task for today and the subsequent 30 days is to compile a list of everything you are grateful for. Take note of every element, whether it's your comfortable couch, air conditioning, coffee, friends, or any other aspects that bring you joy or hold value in your life.

"If you struggle to love yourself, it will be challenging to extend that love to others."

Self-Reflection Notes

Day 15:
Engage in Physical Activity

E ngaging in regular exercise is a way of expressing self-love, given its numerous benefits. Exercise contributes positively to your stress levels, heart and lung health, muscle strength, and metabolism. Additionally, it enhances self-esteem and contributes to a more appealing physical appearance.

Consider enjoyable ways to incorporate exercise into your routine. This could involve scheduling regular walks with a friend, taking up boxing lessons, or indulging in a game of golf.

Consistency in exercise is facilitated by transforming it into a habit. Schedule dedicated time for it, ensuring that you genuinely enjoy the activities you choose. When you find pleasure in your exercise routine, maintaining a regular schedule becomes more achievable.

Reflect on how you can derive enjoyment from exercising and take proactive steps to make it a reality.

"Upon embracing self-love, I embarked on a journey of letting go of all that wasn't beneficial or healthy for me."

"The most extraordinary day of your life is the one when you decide that your life belongs to you. It is a day free from apologies or justifications, where you stop relying on others and release the need to assign blame. The gift of life is solely yours, and it embarks on an incredible journey that you alone are responsible for maintaining its quality. This is the day where your life authentically begins"

Self-Reflection Notes

_____

_____

_____

_____

_____

_____

_____

_____

_____

_____

_____

_____

_____

_____

_____

_____

_____

_____

_____

_____

_____

Day 16:
Refine Your Social Connections

E ach of us has at least one person in our life who shouldn't be there—a friend taking advantage, an ex-partner better kept at a distance, or even a family member consistently mistreating us. It might be as simple as disliking the guy at the deli counter.

- Identify those individuals in your life who don't belong.

- Create a comprehensive list, using a spreadsheet if helpful.

- Arrange them from least to most positive influence.

Begin removing those who contribute negatively until you're left with positive and meaningful connections.

This may involve having a conversation or merely disengaging from certain communications. Take the necessary steps. Recognize your uniqueness; you deserve to have special and positive people in your life.

> **"Seek connections that resonate with mutual respect and genuine understanding."**

Self-Reflection Notes

Day 17:
Engage in Activities You Love

Consider how much of your daily time is devoted to activities you genuinely love.

From the morning rush to work and the commute to the actual work hours, a significant portion of the day slips away without indulging in enjoyable pursuits.

Relying on free time to engage in activities you love is a strategy that often leads to neglecting those activities altogether. The key is to proactively schedule time each day for activities that bring you joy. Recognize that the things you enjoy hold importance because you, in turn, are significant.

Allocate at least 30 minutes today and each day moving forward to engage in something you genuinely enjoy. The nature of the activity is irrelevant; if it brings you joy, that's reason enough to prioritize it.

> "Rather than succumbing to self-pity, it's essential to cultivate a spirit of adventure and embrace the boundless possibilities within oneself."

Self-Reflection Notes

_____

_____

_____

_____

_____

_____

_____

_____

_____

_____

_____

_____

_____

_____

_____

_____

_____

_____

_____

_____

Day 18:
Chart a Course for Your Future

Merely surviving isn't sufficient; that's a level of existence reserved for animals. As a human with the power of choice, take a moment with a cup of coffee or a glass of wine to envision and plan your future. You deserve to manifest the life you envision.

Allow your imagination to soar and craft a compelling vision for the future. Transform your aspirations into a tangible plan on paper.

Crucially, commit to your plan by taking at least one action each day to bring it closer to reality.

Today is the day to take that initial step!

> "Creating a life plan that aligns with your passion, purpose, and personal growth will be rewarding."

Self-Reflection Notes

Day 19:
Maintain a Journal

A Life worth experiencing is worth documenting. By putting pen to paper or typing on a computer, you acknowledge the importance of your life story. Through this practice, you'll gain insights into your actions and recognize areas for improvement that may have escaped your notice. The act of recording itself becomes a catalyst for positive change, as you'll be motivated to engage in meaningful activities worthy of documentation. Whether you opt for the tangible feel of a handwritten journal or the efficiency of a computer, the choice is yours. Commence this meaningful habit today, dedicating a few minutes each night to document your day and thoughts.

"Journaling is an intimate conversation with your soul."

Self-Reflection Notes

_____

_____

_____

_____

_____

_____

_____

_____

_____

_____

_____

_____

_____

_____

_____

_____

_____

_____

_____

Day 20:
Grant Yourself Forgiveness

Certainly, you've made mistakes, and perhaps some were even intentional. Acknowledge that everyone you know, yourself included, has encountered similar experiences. Life is a journey of living and learning. It's crucial to release the burden, forgive yourself, and unburden your conscience.

Extend the compassion you show to others to yourself. Grant forgiveness and liberate yourself from the weight of past errors. Embrace the fact that you have a wonderful life to live, unencumbered by the weight of self-judgment.

> "Forgiveness is a gift that you give yourself, a key to unlocking the chains of self-judgment. In letting go of past mistakes, you can open to selflove, embracing the freedom to create a brighter, more compassionate future within the sanctuary of your heart."

Self-Reflection Notes

_____

_____

_____

_____

_____

_____

_____

_____

_____

_____

_____

_____

_____

_____

_____

_____

_____

_____

_____

Day 21:
Cease the Request for Approval

When you do things to make others view you in a certain way, you're sending a message to yourself that the truth is insufficient. You can be kind, but don't be kind just so others will view you as kind. Just be kind.

There's a significant difference between being a good person and a person who wants to be seen as good.

It's okay if you're a little impatient, or don't like the local NFL team. Be honest about who you are. Everyone who loves you will still be around. Anyone you lose doesn't belong in your life anyway.

Embrace that you're good enough just the way you are. It's a much less exhausting way to live, too.

"When you find yourself standing out from the crowd, it can be easy to overlook the many people who genuinely accept and embrace you for your true self. Instead, it's often the one person who doesn't understand or appreciate you that captures your attention. However, it's important to remember that countless individuals celebrate your uniqueness and see your worth."

Self-Reflection Notes

Day 22:
Spend Time Alone

Some individuals, perhaps even yourself, find it challenging to be alone with their thoughts. They constantly seek external stimuli, such as TV, the internet, car radio, or books, to avoid solitude.

Have you ever questioned why you rely on these distractions? A valuable way to understand this is to take a break from them. When driving alone, try turning off your phone and skipping the radio. Observe your thoughts and reactions during this break.

With consistent practice, you can become an excellent company for yourself. Instead of evading solitude, embrace it. Dedicate at least 10 minutes each day to sit with yourself and uncover what you may discover.

"Alone, you are free to explore the depth of your soul, fostering the profound connection with the most important person - Yourself."

Self-Reflection Notes

_____

_____

_____

_____

_____

_____

_____

_____

_____

_____

_____

_____

_____

_____

_____

_____

_____

_____

_____

_____

Day 23:
Schedule Appointments with your Doctor and Dentist

P rioritizing your health is a clear demonstration of self-love. Take proactive steps by scheduling checkups with your doctor and dentist today. For those already attending to their health, compile a list of five ways to enhance your wellbeing and commit to implementing at least one of them.

"The true essence lies in developing a profound love for oneself and extending that love to someone who truly recognizes and appreciates you. Instead of seeking love as mere compensation for a lack of self-care, prioritize building a strong self-love foundation and then seek a partner who appreciates and reciprocates that love in return."

Self-Reflection Notes

Day 24:
Engage in Volunteer Work

By embracing the act of service, you will uncover a pathway toward a deeper connection with yourself and a heightened sense of joy. In this digital age, countless websites exist to help you explore volunteer opportunities, tailored to your locality. Choose an endeavor close to your heart, invest your time in something meaningful, and witness how even dedicating one hour per week amplifies the love and compassion you hold for yourself. Prepare to be pleasantly surprised as you discover the numerous other benefits waiting to unfold through your volunteering experiences. Curious to know what lies ahead? Take the leap, go volunteer, and embark on your journey to find out.

"Volunteer not merely as a service to the world, but as a gift to your soul the more we contribute, the richer we become in the currency of self-worth."

Self-Reflection Notes

Day 25:
Get Sufficient Rest

Few things have a greater impact on your health, attitude, and happiness than ensuring you get at least seven hours of sleep each night. Even if you believe you function well with only 4-6 hours, try embracing a full seven for a week and observe the changes in your well-being and performance.

Allow yourself to take a nap, sleep in, or go to bed earlier. There are instances when the most loving thing you can do for yourself is to prioritize sleep, even if it means missing a rerun of Purple Rain or Love and Basketball.

Commit today to prioritize seven hours of sleep each night for at least a week.

"A sacred pause that replenishes our spirit is a gift to yourself that you deserve peace and restoration."

Self-Reflection Notes

Day 26:
Establish and Uphold Boundaries

When self-love is lacking, enduring mistreatment becomes a common occurrence. The fear of upsetting others or being disliked often leads to a continuous effort to please everyone, which ultimately proves to be unsuccessful.

Attempting to please everyone results in feelings of resentment and depletion when tolerating things, one doesn't like. The key to resolving this is to learn to say "no" and assertively communicate one's needs. By expressing yourself and setting boundaries, you not only gain the respect of others but also experience an improved sense of self-worth.

"Setting boundaries is a declaration that your well-being matters."

Self-Reflection Notes

Day 27:
Accomplish a Task that You've Been Putting Off

Avoid procrastinating on the important things. Whether it's filing your taxes, going to the dentist, or making a tough phone call, just do it. You lose self-respect and self-esteem when you willingly fail to handle your business.

Today, make a list of the things you've been avoiding and get at least one of them done. Then, focus on how good it felt to get that item completed. Imagine how great you would feel in general if you regularly did whatever needed to be done.

Begin making a habit of listing the things you need to do and then doing them.

"With each completed endeavor, you gift yourself the satisfaction of progress."

Self-Reflection Notes

Day 28:
Rely on Your Instincts

With the wealth of experiences and observations in your life, it's reasonable to assume that you possess substantial knowledge. Your intuition, grounded in these experiences, is a valuable resource.

Starting today, cultivate trust in your intuition, beginning with small decisions. For instance, if you feel an urge to turn right at a stop sign instead of left, follow through and observe the outcome.

When confronted with choices, simply inquire, "Which option is the best for me?" Listen to the answer and act accordingly. This practice allows you to harness the wisdom accumulated throughout your life.

Keep in mind that the most logical solution may not always align with what is truly best for you. Embracing your intuition allows you to leverage your knowledge and experience for your benefit.

"Trust the whispers of your inner wisdom."

Self-Reflection Notes

Day 29:
Engage in Activities that Boost Your Self-Appreciation

Volunteering was one example of this, but there are other things you might think that you should be doing, also. It might be going to church, learning a second language, or meditating for an hour each day.

Think about the characteristics you think a person should have. Make a long list. Now, pick one and start doing it.

You might believe that any self-respecting man should be able to change the oil in his car. Or you might believe that everyone should be able to play a musical instrument. Perhaps you believe everyone should have a decent knowledge of world history.

It doesn't matter what it happens to be. It's entirely up to you. Pick something and begin the process. You'll be thrilled with yourself.

> "The journey of self-love begins by cultivating a genuine liking for oneself. This liking is rooted in self-respect, which flourishes from thinking of oneself in positive and empowering ways."

Self-Reflection Notes

_____

_____

_____

_____

_____

_____

_____

_____

_____

_____

_____

_____

_____

_____

_____

_____

_____

_____

_____

_____

Day 30:
Perform a Kind Act for Someone Anonymously

T his can be an enjoyable and personally fulfilling experience. Select a target, whether it's a neighbor, coworker, or a random stranger, and perform a kind gesture for them.

Whether you choose to mow their grass, send a thoughtful card, or clear the snow off their car, find a way to extend kindness and revel in the positive feelings it brings about.

"A silent declaration that the joy of giving is its reward, creating ripples of fulfillment within."

Self-Reflection Notes

_____

_____

_____

_____

_____

_____

_____

_____

_____

_____

_____

_____

_____

_____

_____

_____

_____

_____

_____

_____

_____

Day 31:
Celebrate Yourself

I n months with 31 days, consider it a bonus opportunity. Indulge in something enjoyable today. Gather a few friends for a bowling outing or head to the deluxe movie theater, treating yourself to that luxurious popcorn.

Embrace a lighthearted and whimsical activity solely because it brings you joy.

"Discover the art of enjoying yourself is a celebration of self-love in its purest form."

Self-Reflection Notes

"Embrace self-love wholeheartedly. Let it motivate you to take the necessary steps towards your happiness.

Embrace the freedom of cutting ties with a past filled with drama.

Choose to set remarkable standards for your relationship, valuing Embracing yourself and seeking connections that uplift and honor
your worth"

The Power of KNOW

Chapter 3

Short Stories

"Keith"

O nce upon a time, in a quiet suburb, there lived a young man named Keith. Keith's life had been marked by a secret that, as he got older, began to sow seeds of curiosity and a longing to be loved by everyone around him.

Keith's mother had an affair with a married man, a relative no less, and as a result, Keith came into existence. Growing up Keith couldn't help but wonder why his mother had made the choices she did. He longed to understand the complexities of love and the consequences that came with it.

As Keith navigated the challenges of adolescence, he carried the weight of his mother's actions on his shoulders. Rejection became a recurring theme in his life, as he couldn't help but question his worth. He yearned to find answers and seek acceptance in a world that seemed to constantly remind him of his origin story.

With each passing day, Keith's desire to comprehend his mother's motivations grew stronger. He knew he couldn't change the past, but he believed that understanding it might help him find peace within himself and foster stronger connections with others.

Keith took it upon himself to have a heart-to-heart conversation with his mother. Tenderly, he approached her with his questions, seeking clarity, understanding, and most importantly, the love he craved. Their conversation was emotional, raw, and filled with moments of vulnerability.

His mother, overwhelmed with guilt and remorse, shared the complexities of her journey and the emotions that clouded her judgment. She explained the flaws and mistakes in her past, all while assuring Keith that his existence was not a reflection of any shortcomings on his part. Instead, she expressed her undying love for him and her sincere regret for the pain she had caused. Through their heart-to-heart, Keith began to realize that his mother's actions, though deeply flawed, did not define who he was as a person. He understood that his worth was not tied to the circumstances of his birth, but rather to how he lived his life and treated others.

With this newfound realization, Keith set out on a journey of self-acceptance and personal growth. He embraced his identity, appreciating the uniqueness of his story and the strength he had gained from it Keith vowed to be compassionate, empathetic, and resilient as he formed connections and fostered love in every relationship he encountered.

As Keith matured, his perspective on rejection transformed. He recognized that his experiences had shaped him into a person who could empathize deeply with others facing their challenges. Keith's ability to convey understanding and acceptance became his greatest strength, allowing him to touch the hearts of those around him.

In the end, Keith's story was not defined by the rejection he faced, but by his journey towards self-discovery and his capacity to love and be loved despite his unconventional background. He showed the world that acceptance begins with oneself and that the power to overcome rejection lies within the depth of understanding, compassion, and personal growth. And so, Keith's life became an inspiration, reminding others that their worth is not determined by the circumstances of their birth, but by their ability to embrace their unique journey and share love with the world.

Keith went on to do some amazing things and helped others with his transformative self-love journey.

"Nicole"

Once upon a time, in a small town nestled amidst rolling green hills, there lived a young girl named Nicole. Nicole was raised by her strong, wise grandmother, who instilled in her the importance of self-love and believing in oneself. Despite her grandmother's guidance, Nicole struggled with her self-image. She was incredibly skinny, shy, and constantly afraid of judgment.

Nicole preferred to stay within the confines of her comfort zone, avoiding interactions with others as much as possible. Her heart yearned for connection and acceptance, but fear held her back. The town she lived in was filled with vibrant individuals, each with their own stories and quirks.

One day, Nicole's uncle came to visit. He was a jovial and kind-hearted man, known for his warm smile and infectious laughter. From the moment he arrived, he could sense Nicole's insecurities and began to make it his mission to uplift her spirit. With gentle words, he encouraged Nicole to step out of her shell and believe in herself. He reminded her that she was somebody special, that her unique voice and presence had the power to make a difference in the world. Although hesitant at first, Nicole slowly began to embrace his message. She realized that self-love was not about changing who she was but rather embracing her true self.

Inspired by her uncle's unwavering support, Nicole decided to face her fears head-on. She joined community activities, engaged in conversations with strangers, and pushed herself to step into the spotlight. With each small victory, her confidence grew, like a flower blossoming in the spring.

As Nicole continued to immerse herself in new experiences, she discovered a writing talent. Channeling her emotions onto paper, she crafted heartfelt stories that resonated with others. Through her words, Nicole shared her journey of self-love, inspiring those who felt lost to believe in their strength and worthiness.

The town became captivated by Nicole's authentic voice, and her stories touched the hearts of many. People began to see beyond her outer appearance, recognizing the wisdom and beauty that radiated from within. Nicole's self-love journey not only transformed her own life but also sparked a newfound sense of acceptance and empathy within the community.

With time, Nicole realized the importance of embracing her physical appearance as well. She saw it as a mere vessel that carried her spirit, and she chose to adorn it with kindness and self-care. Her once frail frame became a symbol of resilience and beauty, a testament to her journey of selflove.

Nicole's story became a beacon of hope for those who struggled with self-doubt and insecurities. Her powerful message rippled through the town, inspiring others to embrace their uniqueness. Nicole's journey taught everyone that self-love was not a destination but rather a lifelong commitment, a constant choice to nourish one's soul and celebrate the beauty of being oneself.

And so, Nicole's story became a reminder, etched in the hearts of all who knew her, that they too were somebody worthy of love, acceptance, and self-belief.

"Octavia"

Once upon a time, there was a little girl named Octavia who grew up feeling a deep sense of loneliness and longing for acceptance. In a house nestled between towering oak trees, she found solace in her imagination, creating a special friend to keep her company. This imaginary friend, whom she named Lily, was a comforting presence, always ready to lend an ear without judgment.

Octavia was a shy and sensitive child, often feeling out of place in social settings. She was quiet, fearing the judgment and rejection that seemed to follow her every step. But when she played with Lily, all those worries disappeared.

Lily became her confidant and ally, a friend who loved her unconditionally and accepted her just as she was.

As Octavia grew older, her reliance on Lily remained, though she kept her imaginary friend a secret from the world. It was Lily who encouraged her to be brave and embrace her uniqueness. Through make-believe adventures and whispered conversations, Lily filled Octavia's heart with selflove and taught her to appreciate the person she was becoming.

One day, as Octavia walked through a bustling park, she noticed a group of children playing nearby. Their laughter and camaraderie enticed her, yet her trepidation held her back. In that moment, she longed for Lily's presence, for the comfort and security she had always provided.

But deep within Octavia's heart, a small flicker of change ignited. She realized that the love and acceptance Lily bestowed upon her was always within her, waiting to be unleashed. With newfound determination, Octavia made a choice: she would share her loving spirit with the world, just as Lily had shared it with her.

Taking small, tentative steps, Octavia began to interact with others, sharing her thoughts and ideas without fear of judgment. She discovered that people were more accepting than she had once imagined. As Octavia opened her heart and allowed herself to be vulnerable, she found that others reciprocated kindness, understanding, and friendship.

Octavia's self-love journey continued to blossom, and her friendship with Lily transformed from a need for acceptance to a symbol of her inner strength and resilience. No longer bound by the walls of her imagination, Octavia realized that she had the power to create connections and love herself wholly.

As the years went by, Octavia's kindness and acceptance of others resonated deeply within her community. She became a beacon of compassion and understanding, radiating the love she had learned from Lily. People were drawn to her warm smile, open heart, and non-judgmental nature.

Octavia's story inspired others to embrace their uniqueness and cherish the power of self-love. She taught them that the acceptance they sought began within themselves, and that true connection with others could only be nurtured by first accepting and loving oneself fully.

And so, Octavia's journey of self-love, once born from a longing for acceptance, became a testimony to the transformative power that lies within every individual. Together with Lily, her imaginary friend turned symbol of self-empowerment, Octavia embarked on a lifelong adventure of compassion, acceptance, and, most importantly, self-love.

"Will"

Once upon a time, in a charming city named Shreveport, there lived a young man named Will. Will was blessed with parents who understood and amplified the importance of self; they actively demonstrated it in their own lives. They were the catalysts that ignited the spark of self-love for him.

From a young age, Will's parents instilled in him the belief that loving oneself was not only a luxury but a necessity. They taught him that selflove meant accepting and embracing every facet of his being, celebrating his strengths, and tenderly acknowledging his flaws.

Will wholeheartedly absorb this wisdom. He began incorporating self-love practices into his daily routine, recognizing his worth and taking time for himself. Each morning, he stood before the mirror, speaking affirmations that sealed his self-belief. "I am worthy. I am deserving of love. I am enough."

His authentic self-love radiated from within, attracting positivity and people who resonated with his empowering energy. Will found solace in gratitude, appreciating the simple joys of life and expressing thanks for the blessings that encompassed his world.

As he continued along his journey of self-love, Will understood that nurturing himself went together with extending kindness to others. He lent a helping hand whenever he could, offering support and comfort to those in need.

However, he learned the importance of setting boundaries and prioritizing his well-being. Will understood that self-love meant committing to his growth and happiness. He engaged in activities that brought him joy, be it pursuing hobbies, meditating amidst nature's embrace, or simply indulging in moments of solitude. He recognized that by making himself a priority, he could better serve others, exuding love from an abundant heart.

Throughout his life, Will embodied the essence of self-love. It became his guiding principle, sculpting his interactions and shaping his journey. He flourished, radiating compassion, confidence, and inner peace.

In the end, Will's story was not just about selflove; it was a testament to the boundless beauty and strength that blossomed from within when one embraced their worth. Will inspired others to honor themselves, accept themselves fully, and remember that they too deserved the love and care they freely gave to others.

And so, Will's life became a shining example, igniting a wave of self-love and inner happiness in the hearts of all those touched by his gentle spirit. He demonstrated that by nurturing oneself, setting boundaries, and making self-care a priority, we not only fill our cups but overflow with love and compassion for the world around us.

Chapter 4

Self-Love Affirmations

I am somebody.

I can do it.

I am enough.

I am deserving.

I can have it.

I am beautiful (or I am handsome).

I am healthy.

I am a conqueror.

I am worthy of love and acceptance just as I am.

I deserve happiness and fulfillment in my life.

I embrace my uniqueness and celebrate my authentic self.

I am enough, exactly as I am at this moment.

I honor my needs and prioritize self-care in my daily routine.

I release self-judgment and replace it with compassion and understanding.

I am deserving of forgiveness, both from others and myself.

I radiate love and positivity, attracting the same into my life.

I trust in my abilities and have confidence in my decision-making.

I am resilient and capable of overcoming challenges with grace.

I choose to love and accept myself unconditionally, beyond any flaws or imperfections.

I give myself permission to prioritize my wellbeing and make myself a priority.

I am worthy of all the love, joy, and abundance that life has to offer.

I embrace my journey of self-discovery and growth, trusting that I am always evolving into my best self.

I deserve to be treated with kindness, respect, and understanding in all my relationships.

I am grateful for every part of myself, including my strengths, weaknesses, and everything in between.

I let go of comparison and embrace my unique path, knowing that I am enough just as I am. I am worthy of setting healthy boundaries that honor and protect my emotional well-being. I choose to forgive myself for past mistakes and allow love and compassion to guide me forward. I am my own biggest supporter, believing in myself and my ability to achieve my dreams.

I am enough just as I am.

I will be kind to myself as I am kind to others.

I will nurture myself like I nurture others.

I will be optimistic about my life as I am about others' life.

I know that I am worthy like others are worthy.

I know the Power of KNOW.
I embrace the Power of KNOW.

Conclusion

Congratulations that you know to KNOW! You've successfully transformed your self-perception over the past month.

Reflect on the following:

- How do you currently feel compared to the initial day? What is your self-love and selfesteem rating now?

- Considering you've maintained a journal for weeks, what transformations do you notice in your entries over time?

- Have any of the activities become ingrained as habits?

- What steps can you take in the future to continue enhancing your self-love?

Take pride in your accomplishments. Thirty days of cultivating self-love is a significant achievement, albeit just a small stride in a larger journey.

Remember, the journey towards maximum selflove may span a lifetime, but the positive news is that life becomes more enjoyable as you deepen your self-appreciation.

You've realized that societal values don't define your worth; you can set your standards. Your ability to value yourself and progress toward your vision of a good person is what truly matters.

When you believe in your continual improvement, satisfaction with yourself follows naturally.

Start contemplating how to proceed from this new starting point. This marks the initial phase of the incredible future awaiting you!

How do you currently feel compared to the initial day? What is your self-love and self-esteem rating now?

Considering you've maintained a journal for weeks, what transformations do you notice in your entries over time?

Have any of the activities become ingrained as habits?

What steps can you take in the future to continue enhancing your self-love?

_____

_____

_____

_____

_____

_____

_____

_____

_____

_____

_____

_____

_____

_____

_____

_____

"The Power of KNOW:

Be Kind, Nurturing, Optimistic

and

Worthy to Self."

Made in the USA
Middletown, DE
02 September 2024

60277084R00066